Healing Prayers for Depression

Rev. Dr. Durrell Watkins

ISBN 978-0-557-86515-4

Published in 2010 by Lulu

For information, contact Durrell Watkins, 1480 SW Ninth Ave., Fort Lauderdale, FL 33315 (Durrell@sunshinecathedral.net)

Contents

Remember:

Only a licensed therapist is qualified to offer on-going professional counseling. Only a physician can diagnose medical conditions or prescribe medication for illnesses. Support groups, chatting with friends, spiritual direction, self-help books and even prayer are all excellent complementary tools for your healing process, but only the appropriate licensed professionals can diagnose and properly treat health (including mental health) conditions. This book isn't meant to be used to diagnose depression, and never is the suggestion made that this book alone can cure depression. This is a book of prayer meant to encourage and comfort you as you access all the appropriate support systems to help you return to a life of health and joy.

Healing Prayers for Depression

**[1]I will lift up mine eyes unto the hills, from whence
cometh my help. [2]My help cometh from the LORD,
which made heaven and earth. [7]The LORD shall
preserve thee from all evil: [God] shall preserve thy
soul. [8]The LORD shall preserve thy going out and thy
coming in from this time forth, and even for evermore.
(*Psalm 121, AV*)**

Depression is a medical condition which can be treated. If you are experiencing symptoms of depression, you should tell your physician and see if there is a medical treatment that would be appropriate for you. You may want to consider seeing a licensed psychotherapist as well. There are self-help books that may be useful to you, and support groups, too. You will find suggestions throughout this book meant to encourage you on your healing journey. If you are suffering from depression, you definitely will want to get the help and support you need, and the good news is there is help available to you.

As a person of faith, I believe that prayer is also a valuable tool in any healing plan. So, in addition to support groups, therapists, and prescribed medications, I would encourage people battling depression to include prayer in their daily lives as they try to move through their illness and reclaim their power and their joy.

See the professionals and follow their advice. Lean on supportive friends and never be embarrassed to ask for help. And spend time each day in prayer; ask the God of your understanding to comfort you, strengthen you, guide you, and to help you find your way back to a life of happiness and fulfillment.

This book offers one prayer for each day of the month with a few extra at the end. Use the prayer that seems to address the issue you want to work on in any given day, or simply go through the book using the prayer assigned to the current day of the month.

Pray in the morning, or pray at night, or both. Pray with a prayer partner, or during a time of intentional holy Silence in private. Pray once a day or throughout the day. What is most important is that you come to believe that you are not alone, that you are a person of sacred value, and that good things are possible for you. So keep praying and keep doing all the work you need to do to feel and be your best, because you really are worth it!

Bright Blessings,

Durrell

Rev. Dr. Durrell Watkins
Sunshine Cathedral, Fort Lauderdale

A Personal Story

The reason I wanted to write this book is because I have suffered from depression. I am probably at least the third generation in my family to suffer from depression. In fact, in three generations of both the paternal and maternal sides of my family, I can identify no fewer than five people who have battled depression throughout their lives. Were they depressed because of events in their formative years or was their depression hereditary? I don't have answers to those questions; however, I am the first (and to my knowledge only) person in my family to seek professional help for the condition, and I know that getting the help one needs is much better than needlessly going it alone.

My childhood was a consistently unhappy experience for me, full of fear and shame. Depression is common for people who survived abuse as children; I don't need to give details, blame anyone, or turn this small book into a tell-all, but I can say that depression started early in my life and left scars at the soul level that have troubled me off and on throughout my life.

In addition to experiencing dysfunctional family dynamics, I was also "different" in a rural, bible-belt community that was openly hostile to "different" (gay) people like me. Childhood was complex, and frankly, I don't miss a day of it. Melancholia was a much more frequent visitor in my early life than was happiness.

I eventually tried to numb the pain of depression with the usual tools from the survival kit I had constructed over time: denial, secret keeping, sexually acting out, drug experimentation, and excessive drinking. But I was already in the habit of numbing feelings before I realized that is what I was doing.

One semester in college, I dropped all but one course, worked as little as possible to keep my part-time job, and spent the first half or more of the spring semester rarely leaving my home and sometimes not even getting dressed for days at a time. A friend who noticed my pseudo-hibernation said, "Those are symptoms of depression." And so they were.

Though I started college with a bang (making the President's and Dean's lists), I finished in five and a half years (rather than four) with a less than stellar Grade Point Average.

I took my degree and my low self-esteem and moved to the big city. After a few failed relationships, a few disappointing jobs, a few failed attempts at therapy, bouts of binge drinking and being diagnosed with a chronic (but eventually treatable) health condition, I finally made a full commitment to therapy and spent the next several months doing the hard work of healing. I also started taking medication for depression with excellent results for about ten years.

I moved to the bigger city (with a couple of suburban stops along the way) and found my joy. I excelled as a graduate student (earning two masters' degrees and a doctorate degree), succeeded as an interdisciplinary artist, began what has been the longest romantic relationship of my life (over a decade and still going), and fulfilled a dream of writing books.

During this Renaissance period in my life, there were changes and losses (including the deaths of both my grandmothers), but I was able to move through my grief and I appreciated the support of wonderful friends and colleagues. In fact, a dear spiritual advisor held my hand and my heart during the loss of my maternal grandmother, and I am forever indebted to Rev. Pat Bumgardner for her friendship, mentorship, and unrestricted kindness during that time.

With a commitment to doing what brought joy to my heart, with the support of wonderful friends, and with effective medication, my mental health remained stable.

Then, I moved to the Southeast for an amazing career opportunity. The tropical weather and the career advancement were very exciting, but leaving close friends behind (as well as a thriving arts scene) along with the stress that accompanies any major move took its toll. Stress started building over time, and in January of 2010 my father died.

My father and I never really "bonded" and our relationship evolved from hostile to distant to awkwardly polite to an honest, if rarely articulated, mutual understanding and respect. That's a lot of progress in 43 years, but we never quite got to "close." His death represented the end of any possibility of such closeness existing, and of course, there were regrets about what never really was. He probably loved me more than I ever knew, and for that matter, I probably loved him more than I ever knew, but the chance to do more with that revelation ended with his demise. Normal grief followed.

However, as the year progressed and stressful situations presented themselves to me, I found myself becoming more and more fatigued and feeling more and more isolated and lonely. It was a year of conflict, changes, loss, setbacks, and discouragement. There were also many blessings, but when one is overwhelmed by challenges, blessings are sometimes not as obvious as they would be at other times.

When a friend I had tried to lean on for support during this difficult time told me he was moving away, the fear of loss and a sense of loneliness consumed me and I went into a deep, dark depression that lasted for many months. Though a loved one moving away, in hindsight, may not seem like the end of the world, it was the straw that broke my fragile peace of mind. It was one loss in a year of repeated losses and disappointments too many.

It was time to get help once again. The dis-ease of depression was back.

I turned to friends. I turned to a spiritual director. I turned to more friends. I leaned on my life-partner. I received a medical evaluation and had my medications changed. I went back into therapy. I took a vacation (and then another), and I began exercising daily. I looked into support groups. And, of course, I prayed.

With so much effort, I expected the depression to lift magically, instantly, almost effortlessly. But no such instant miracle took place.

As I meditated, cried, prayed, attempted to “talk it out and walk it out” (a phrase my therapist used for expressing my feelings and staying physically active), I would improve, and then flounder.

After weeks of sadness and anxiety, I experienced two and a half good days in a row! It was followed by two weeks of misery. Then I experienced eight good days in a row! It was followed by a week-long relapse. And then I realized what I had been missing.

You see, I had done the work to figure out what childhood events caused me to develop the *habit* of feeling unloved or unsafe or unwanted. I had learned the biological reasons that my brain might need medical assistance to produce all the chemicals it needed, in the right amounts, for me to have balanced emotions. I even explored the need for better self-care, and I had to understand that a lot of stressful events really had occurred in my life in a short amount of time. But all that "understanding" and all the work I was doing wasn't turning my emotional ship around. And that is because, I was still imagining myself as a victim of my emotions.

Habits can be developed in just three weeks, and I had certainly spent more than three weeks focusing on what was wrong more than on what was right, on what I had lost rather than on what I still had, and on what had been difficult rather than on what was still possible. And, as I have known for years and have preached and written about time and again, what we focus on, we will drift toward, create or attract. I was focusing on feeling lonely and unappreciated, and as my focus remained on that negative condition, more and more situations popped up to confirm my isolation.

Rather than just feeling my feelings without judging them, I was resisting them and viewing myself as somehow deficient for having them. By struggling against the feelings rather than simply noticing them without judgment, I was perpetuating misery in my own life. And, as I clung to misery, people and events continued to show up to validate my misery. I seemed to attract betrayal, insensitivity, loss, and disappointment. What I continued to think about I continued to bring about; focusing on my misery fueled more misery.

Then I remembered what I really always knew...what we focus on creates feelings, and feelings produce an emotional frequency and situations tend to gravitate to matching frequencies. "According to your belief, it is done unto you." My habitual thinking was creating feelings which were creating a frequency which attracted corresponding situations.

As long as I focused on my misery, I was bound to attract or create more misery. Only taking responsibility for my own thinking could change my experience. Depression was my "dis-ease" - not someone else's responsibility to correct for me.

I'm not saying I deserved to be unhappy, or that others never made mistakes that hurt me, or that sadness isn't a valid emotional response to loss. But blaming others for my pain, or even blaming myself for experiencing appropriate, natural emotions, never brought joy or healing to my experience of life. Releasing judgment and loving myself were what would serve me better.

No one could mend my emotions for me; the work was mine to do. There were kind and loving people to help and support me, but I had to do the work of healing for myself.

The instant I realized that I was contributing to my own experience by my habitual focus, I made a decision to redirect my focus. I started giving thanks for my dear friends who were trying to care for me during my time of sadness.

I started giving what I wanted to get. I began offering support and kindness to others who were going through a hard time. Almost immediately, people who had no idea that I had been suffering were telling me how important I was to them, how they felt drawn to me, and how my reaching out to them made a real difference for them. People started “demonstrating” love for me; I wasn’t alone! I never had been.

This realization that I had the power to choose my focus which could change my feelings which would change how I perceived reality was important, but I also realized that healing is often a process. I made a decision to not make things worse by condemning myself for taking months to remember what I really had always known.

I decided to be gentle with myself rather than feeling embarrassed for having shown my need and frailty during a difficult time. I decided to be grateful for those who stood by me offering me almost daily or weekly words of encouragement and demonstrations of love, as well as for those who did so only once or twice, and I even chose to believe that those who couldn’t give me support during my time of crisis were probably doing the best that they could, and maybe making more of an effort than I could let myself acknowledge. And even if they weren't, that was their issue, not mine. My issue was to love myself, give myself the time I needed to heal, and know that things could indeed get better for me.

I decided to be grateful that the healing realization came, however long it took. The miracle was my change of perception; how and when that change of perception manifested as better feelings and conditions in my life, only time would tell. But the healing began the very instant I allowed myself to love and forgive myself, when (as *A Course in Miracles* teaches), I remembered I could *choose again.*

I decided to be grateful for therapists and friends and my dear life-partner and for medications and for time which allowed the healing process to work: as St. Paul once wisely noticed, "All things work together for good..."

There were many contributors to my healing moment and rather than judging myself for not getting it sooner,

I simply decided to rejoice that it happened at all.

Therapy, medication, peer support, and prayer helped me retake control of my thinking, and once again I was able to know that when we change our thinking we change our lives. If we need help to change our thinking, thankfully that help is available!

Clergy get depressed. Therapists get depressed. Nurses get depressed. Smart people get depressed. Fun people get depressed. I've learned that throughout history, some of the politicians, religious leaders, positive thinkers, entrepreneurs, healers, and celebrities I have admired most also went through periods of depression. Maybe being so dedicated to their work opened the door to imbalance for them. Maybe being sensitive (which is what drew them to public service or to healing or to the arts) meant that they would sometimes experience the sad times much more deeply than others. Maybe depression was their gift; having worked through depression, however many times, they could then offer healing because they had personally needed and experienced healing themselves. In any case, depression is not something that we need to be ashamed of, nor is it something about which we must remain hopeless.

My story is just my own. As you work your steps, go through psychoanalysis, and seek medical treatment, you will come to your own breakthroughs. For me, forgiving myself and others was a way of reclaiming my power and beginning to return to a place of joy. And until I got there, prayer helped to sustain me along the way. Prayer helped me love myself more, and love is always a healing power!

I offer you the prayers, suggestions, and my personal story in this book as a testimony that healing is possible; and if once healed you find yourself depressed again down the road, healing is possible again. Love yourself through it, and love yourself enough to get the help you need, and when you get better, you may just want to share your story to help encourage others too. “We are as sick as our secrets.” I decided to come out of the depression closet, and as with most coming out experiences, the perceived risks are outweighed (for me) by the hope and the empowerment that follow.

I offer you now, with love and hope, *Healing Prayers for Depression.*

Day 1

I Get To Choose What I See

I look out my window and what do I see?

Clouds? They are the divine presence watching lovingly over me.

Sunlight? That is the light of joy filling my heart.

Rain? That is heavenly grace washing away all sadness and anxiety.

Snow? That is a blanket of beauty covering my life.

Storms? That is the exuberant dance of life celebrating my very existence.

I look around today, and whatever I see is an affirmation of my sacred value and it brings a smile to my face.
And so it is!

“All shall be well, all shall be well, and all manner of things shall be well.”
Julian of Norwich

SELF-TALK

What I focus on I will drift toward, create or attract! Today I will focus on what makes my heart glad.

Day 2

Self Love, Forgiveness, and Healing

If I have allowed myself to feel unloved, unimportant, unworthy, or disconnected from the eternal, omnipresent spirit of Life, I will remind myself that Love is all there is.

If I have felt needy, rather than judging myself, I will love and bless myself, knowing that my true Self has no unmet needs at all.

If I have felt lonely or scared, rather than condemning myself, I will put my hand on my heart and look into the mirror and declare, "I love you. Unconditionally and forever, I love you."

If I have felt abandoned or betrayed, I will know today that God has never left me, never would, never could; and God can show up for me in infinite ways: a lover, a friend, a companion, a pet, a therapist, a good neighbor, or the creativity of the arts are all ways that God is made manifest in my life.

God is constantly expressing in, through, as, and all around me and God is Love and the Love that God is can heal all wounds, real or imagined, old or new.

I let go of shame, blame, fear, regret, and self-pity right now and I allow the miracle I need to flow into my experience.

If I need the miracle to be repeated tomorrow, or if I need a new one, that's OK. There is no shortage of miracles. There is no limit to the miracles I can receive.

I am comforted, encouraged, empowered, and renewed. Alleluia!
Thank you God!
Amen.

SELF-TALK

What I focus on I will drift toward, create or attract! Today I will focus on the love that I Am.

Day 3

I AM

I am starlight.
I am love.
I am energy.
I am eternal wisdom.
I am one with infinite compassion.
I am one with all life.
I am connected to all beings in and beyond the universe.
I am part of the omnipresent, everlasting web of existence.

When I consider what I really am, I am encouraged.

I am optimistic.
I am grateful.
I am unwilling to give up on my happiness.
I am unwilling to give up on myself.

I am no less a miracle than the Big Bang, than gravity or air, than childbirth or first love.

Today I remind myself of what I really am, and I choose to live into the Greatness that I Am.

And so it is that all is well.

Why not watch a funny movie today?

SELF-TALK

What I focus on I will drift toward, create or attract! Today I will focus on what makes my heart glad.

Day 4

Angel Friends

Angels are holding me, watching over me, smiling on me, wishing me well, seeing the best in me, sharing my sorrows and celebrating my joys.

Whether angels are the better parts of my human nature, my highest ideals, my fondest imaginings, beautiful memories, energy centers in my body, the ancestors, spirit guides, loving friends, adoring pets, or kind strangers, I give thanks for their presence in my life.

I depend on and am grateful for the ministry of angels.
I know that I am never really alone.
Amen.

Some people may not understand your depression because it isn't something you can point to like an arm in a cast or a bruised knee. Don't take their lack of understanding personally. Their limited understanding is not your failure. There are people who do understand, and even those who don't may still be wishing you all the best. There is more support available to you than you may have so far realized.

SELF-TALK

What I focus on I will drift toward, create or attract! Today I will focus on what makes my heart sing.

Day 5

There is Help

Self-help books.

Loving friends.
Support groups.
Professional counselors.

Medication.
Meditation.
Exercise.
Rest.

The beauty of nature.
Laughter that breaks out in spite of sadness.
A wise or comforting comment from a neighbor, co-worker, or stranger.

There are so many ways that Life is supporting me, offering me encouragement, reminding me that healing is possible and that there is reason to hope.

There is plenty of help for me; there is healing for me.

For all the ways that my joy is being renewed, I give thanks and I allow it to be.
Amen.

SELF-TALK

What I focus on I will drift toward, create or attract! Today I will focus on all for which I am grateful.

Day 6

My Divine Source

God is my Source, and my Source is infinite and infinitely capable of meeting my every need.

I am now asking my divine Source to comfort me, strengthen me, and fill me with wisdom and love.

I am choosing to trust in this moment that blessings are flowing into my experience of life.

In the name of Jesus and of all helpers of humanity, I declare that all is well in my life, and so it is.
Amen.

Self-talk is very powerful. Tell yourself something affirming and uplifting right now! Say out loud something you are thankful for, something you like about yourself, or something fun you are looking forward to doing in the near future.

SELF-TALK

What I focus on I will drift toward, create or attract! Today I will focus on my best qualities.

Day 7

Today's Gift

This day has a gift for me.

Something good is mine to experience today.
I'm open to it.
I will recognize it, receive it, and be grateful for it.

Nothing can keep my wonderful gift from me.
And so it is.

What is one of the successes you've had in your life? Did you come in first or second in a competition? Are you a good care-giver to a pet? Are you a good gardener or do you cook well? Can you play an instrument? Do you have an interesting laugh? Do you read really fast? What is something that you are very good at and for which you can praise yourself? There IS something!

SELF-TALK

What I focus on I will drift toward, create or attract! Today I will focus on something good in my past, or something good in my present, or something good I'm hoping to experience in the future.

Day 8

Sowing & Reaping Happiness

Mother-Father God,
You who are throughout the universe,
throughout the multiverse,

We ask you for blessings,
aware that to be blessed is to be happy.

Give us the courage to be happy!
Help us to love ourselves enough that
we allow ourselves to be happy.

Give us the grace to wish all people lives
of happiness and well-being.

Give us generosity so that we may
share freely of ourselves to help others
be happy.

And as we sow seeds of joy, let us
expect a bountiful harvest of the same;
it is in your many names that we pray.
Amen.

"The season of failure is the best time to sow the seeds of success." Paramahansa Yogananda

SELF-TALK

What I focus on I will drift toward, create or attract! Today I will focus on what makes my heart glad.

Day 9

Trusting the Healing Process

When there is a good moment, a happy event, a pleasant thought, a joyous memory, an opportunity to laugh, I will recognize it, savor it, and give thanks for it.

I am becoming more balanced, more focused, and more optimistic every day.

I am not condemning myself when my healing feels slow, but I am choosing to believe that the healing process is at work.

Feelings come and go, but my sacred value is constant and the power of life within me is leading me in the direction of happiness and wholeness.

Life is supporting me as I find my way. Divine order is being established in my life and I affirm that ultimately, all is well. I am thankful and so it is.

Dare to hope that things will get better.

SELF-TALK

What I focus on I will drift toward, create or attract! Today I will focus on reasons for hope.

Day 10

Renewed Joy

Deliverer of the despondent,
Friend of the forgotten,
Healer of hurting hearts,
Mender of mournful minds,
Savior of sorrowful souls,
Spirit of abundant life,

I pray for those who are feeling morose, troubled, sad, lonely, or discontent.

Lift them up.
Comfort and console them.
Let a gentle shower of blessings fall continuously into their lives.

May they know there is an everlasting Love that now holds them, fills them, flows through them, and is seeking always to bring them hope, health, and happiness.

May the gift of joy be renewed in their lives and in every life. Amen.

Congratulate yourself for doing the work that will help you heal.

SELF-TALK

What I focus on I will drift toward, create or attract! Today I will focus on the good work I'm doing in the healing process.

Day 11

Wholeness

In the story of Jesus feeding a multitude in the desert, he had his disciples gather up the fragments of what was left.

May the Lord of my life/ Goddess of my being help me gather up any fragments of myself that I have left somewhere, so that I may reintegrate all parts into a renewed, healthy, and joyful whole. Amen.

Get out of the house. Go to the mall, to a movie, to the gym, to the park, the zoo, or a museum. If you can't get out, find something fun to watch on television or listen to your favorite music. Just have a few minutes of fun right now.

SELF-TALK

What I focus on I will drift toward, create or attract! Today I will focus on the idea of wholeness.

Day 12

Hope

When the road is dark and the outcome is uncertain,

when the night seems as if morning may never come,

when the shadows present themselves as monsters, and the winds sound like goblins at our backs,

when sleep won't come and food loses its taste,

when water fails to refresh and joy becomes a long lost friend,

remind us, O God, that Hope still dwells within us.

Give us the strength to hold up our heads, the courage to move forward, and the grace to believe that blessings are on the way.

And when we no longer can help ourselves, let your angels come to our aid. Amen.

Prayer really does help. Prayer, medical treatment, counseling, staying active...it all works together for your benefit. Keep up the good work!

SELF-TALK

What I focus on I will drift toward, create or attract! Today I will focus on the comfort that prayer provides.

Day 13

A Short Prayer for Myself & Others

I affirm blessings today for my life and for all who are dear to me.

Why not reach out to someone today? A co-worker, a friend, a neighbor, even a stranger on a help-line or a prayer ministry? Email someone, call someone, spend 5 minutes talking to someone. Go to the library and read a magazine and smile at people when they walk by, or go to the market and buy an orange and spend a few seconds speaking to the person at the register. Just spend a few pleasant moments interacting with someone today.

SELF-TALK

What I focus on I will drift toward, create or attract! Today I will focus on the truth that I have gifts to share.

Day 14

The Power to Choose

With my thoughts and actions I am choosing from an infinite field of possibilities the experiences I will have today.

I have the power to demonstrate well-being, harmony, success, and fulfillment, and so I choose to do so. For my Good, I am thankful. Amen.

Remember a happy moment. Feel the happiness of that moment again. Be grateful that you have this beautiful memory. Know that more happiness is possible.

SELF-TALK

What I focus on I will drift toward, create or attract! Today I will focus on the power I have to direct my mind. My mind, being part of the One Mind, can accomplish whatever I tell it to do. Today, I'm telling it to be glad and grateful.

Day 15

Gratitude

Dear God,
I give thanks for the blessings that are mine today,
for peaceful rest that will come throughout the night,
and for your divine assistance with all I do tomorrow.
Amen.

"The most common way people give up their power is by thinking they don't have any."
Alice Walker

SELF-TALK

What I focus on I will drift toward, create or attract! Today I will focus on the blessings I've had, the blessings I have, and the blessings I continue to hope for. As I focus on blessings, I am drifting toward, creating, or attracting more blessings!

Day 16

Love

Divine Love,
I am willing today to love myself more.

I am willing to allow love into my life more abundantly.

I am willing to believe that I deserve love, and that I have love to share with my world.

I recognize now that I am enfolded in your embrace and wonderful blessings are mine to experience today;
and so I am thankful, receptive, and full of joy. Amen.

Move. Take a walk. Clap your hands. Take a deep breath. Stretch. Smile. Just do something simple and positive right now.

SELF-TALK

What I focus on I will drift toward, create or attract! Today I will focus on creating the right kind of relationship with myself. As I love myself, I will love others more; and as I give love, I will receive more love. It all begins with loving myself.

Day 17

My Best Self

Let blessings pour into my life like a gentle and long lasting rain.

Let healing blow through my life like a strong and refreshing wind.

Let joy fill my life like a spring-fed pond.

Let peace fill my life like the miracle of the dawn.

Let wisdom guide my life like a bright, shining star.

Let me be my best self, enjoying communion with my True Self, today and every day. Amen.

Have you read a good book lately
(other than this one of course!)?
Read something enjoyable soon.

SELF-TALK

What I focus on I will drift toward, create or attract! Today I will focus on my right to have fun!

Day 18

I Am Safe

Loving Source of peace and hope and joy,

I am trusting you today to guide me in the ways of blessing and to fill me with light.

With your help, I will accomplish my goals with ease and I will know that there is always Good for me to have, to enjoy, and to share.

In your embrace I am safe and secure and I can affirm that all is well.
And so it is.

Let your sadness go down the drain! If you can't shake off that "icky" feeling, then take a shower and imagine all the gloom falling away from you as the soap and water slide down your body. "See" all the sadness just swirling down the drain. Now you are fresh and clean, inside and out!

SELF-TALK

What I focus on I will drift toward, create or attract! Today I will focus on feeling safe in and with the God of my understanding.

Day 19

Trust

Goddess/ God, Eternal Spirit,
Sometimes we don't know how to pray.
Sometimes we don't know what to ask for, what to hope for, what to work for.
Sometimes we need direction, or comfort, or the courage to simply not know.

Sometimes we need to trust that it's all working out, even when we can't predict how, and we need to remember that the universe is unfolding exactly as it should.

And so, Holy One,
Let us trust in grace equal to every need today.

Let us trust that ultimately, all is well.

Let us know that we are on a journey that is right for us.

Let us have peace within, and moments

of true joy that we cherish and share. And may we dare to believe that our Good is always at hand. Amen.

Offer support to someone who could use it today. You can be a blessing to someone, and that always feels good!

SELF-TALK

What I focus on I will drift toward, create or attract! Today I will focus on all that I can trust in my life.

Day 20

May I Be Blessed

God of many names,
in this new moment of this new day,
may I be renewed and filled with hope
and happiness and a sense of purpose.

May I know that I am one with all life.

May I remember that I am a person of sacred value.

May I be confident, courageous, self-realized and Self-realized.

May I be receptive to all the Good that is available to me.

May I live as one who is truly blessed,
And may I be a blessing to others.
Amen.

Give yourself a break. Be patient with yourself. If your healing isn't instant, don't beat yourself up. It's a process. Praise yourself for the good days, the good moments. Give yourself the time it takes to heal. Be gentle with yourself.
You deserve it.

SELF-TALK

What I focus on I will drift toward, create or attract! Today I will focus on what makes my heart glad.

Day 21

The Divine Will

*God within us,
you offer all that is needed for a joyous and worthwhile life.*

Harmonious relationships, peace, happiness, prosperity, good health and success are available to each of us.

Your heavenly will is for each of us to live abundantly and so we pray, "thy will be done on earth as it is in heaven," which means, let us experience the perfection that you are in every area of our lives.

And so it is with confidence, gratitude, and joyful expectation that we release this prayer treatment to the activity of the law of Mind and we trust that all is well. Amen.

Laugh out loud. Right now; just do it.
Even if it feels insincere, just laugh.
Tee hee. What could it hurt? And, after all, it's free!

SELF-TALK

What I focus on I will drift toward, create or attract! Today I will focus on every good thing in my life, no matter how small it may seem. There is good in my life and today I notice and appreciate my good.

Day 22

Word Power

I use the power of my word today to focus my thoughts and intentions only on what is good and desirable. What I focus on, I will drift toward, create, or attract.

By being intentional with the words I speak and the thoughts I entertain, I am choosing to feel good and I am creating the kind of day and the kind of life that I deserve and desire.

I focus on what is good, hopeful, beautiful, loving, creative, joyous, and abundant; blessings flow freely into my experience today.
I demand it!
I allow it!
I give thanks for it!

And so it is.

"I could see peace instead of this."
A Course in Miracles

SELF-TALK

What I focus on I will drift toward, create or attract! Today I will focus on what makes my heart glad.

Day 23

A Blessed Day

May this day bring us peace and joy.
May this day bring us love and prosperity.

May this day find our dear ones well.
May this day see merciful justice prevail.

May this day be a wonderful day filled with blessings.
Amen.

Churches/spiritual centers often offer Tai Chi or Yoga lessons, meditation groups, Taize services, Centering Prayer, spiritual direction, or Metaphysics classes. These are opportunities to deepen spiritual practice, meet nice people, and develop habitual positive thinking.

SELF-TALK

What I focus on I will drift toward, create or attract! Today I will focus on what makes my heart sing.

Day 24

One With All Good

The illusion of separation from Good is now being dispelled.

Divine Love is all-encompassing and can have no opposite.
Alleluia! Amen.

There are people who can help. Psychologists, psychiatrists, physicians, social workers, support groups, ministers, rabbis, teachers, friends...there are people who can help. Please let them.

SELF-TALK

What I focus on I will drift toward, create or attract! Today I will focus on the idea that I am one with All Good.

Day 25

Receptive to Good

I abide in a consciousness of joy.
I abide in a consciousness of abundance.

I abide in a consciousness of health.
I abide in a consciousness of peace.

I choose this day to be happy and poised and grateful for all the Good that I see and even for unknown blessings that are already on their way into my experience.

I declare this to be a divine order day and I allow it to be.

Divine energies are flowing through my life, leading me in the ways of wisdom, and drawing to me all that I need to feel accomplished, safe, and opulently prospered.

All is well in my world today, and so I am thankful and I am receptive to my Good. Amen.

If you have had a difficult time, others have too; and if any of them got through it, you can too!

SELF-TALK

What I focus on I will drift toward, create or attract! Today I will focus on stories of people who have healed, recovered, or successfully started over; I will remind myself that others have improved and I can too.

Day 26

Essence of Life

Eternal Essence of Life within me, I acknowledge your presence expressing in, through, and as my life.

I trust that you are guiding me always to wonderful opportunities, helping me to see and seize the possibilities around me.

I allow you now to erase from me all fear, all regret, all belief in lack or limitation, all false notions of inadequacy, scarcity, or separation from you.

In the place of these error thoughts, let me now be filled with hope and joyful expectation of Good.

Let me now demand and accept the blessings of health, happiness, success, supply, peace, wisdom, and love.

As I am blessed, let me be a blessing to others and may all people come to know of their unity with you.

I feel your presence within me, and I am made whole, perfect, and complete. This is my truth and for it I rejoice.

Let the power of hope bless your life.

SELF-TALK

What I focus on I will drift toward, create or attract! Today I will focus on the experiences I've had or witnessed or imagined of hope, peace, love, and joy.

Day 27

My Truth

God's goodness is my Truth.
God's unconditional love is my experience.
Amen.

Depression is a medical condition
that can be medically treated.
There is nothing to be embarrassed about.
Get the help you need and start feeling better.

SELF-TALK

What I focus on I will drift toward, create or attract! Today I will focus on what makes my heart glad.

Day 28

Everlasting Omnipresence

The Source and Substance of all life is eternal and omnipresent.
It is expressing through and as me and so I am one with all life, now and forever.

No blame. No shame. It's not your fault. Feelings are just feelings. They come and go. When they become overwhelming, there are professionals who can help us get back on track. Be grateful there is help for you, and let yourself receive the help you need and deserve.

SELF-TALK

What I focus on I will drift toward, create or attract! Today I will focus on all the help that is available to me.

Day 29

Uplifted

I am uplifted and I am an uplifting presence in the world.

"Be kind to yourself.
Begin to love and approve
of yourself."
Louise Hay

Is CoDA (Codependent Anonymous, a 12 Step group dedicated to developing healthier relationships) appropriate for you? How about Al-Alon (for friends and family members of problem drinkers)? Adult Children of Alcoholics (a 12 Step group for women and men who grew up in alcoholic or otherwise dysfunctional homes)? There is also Emotions Anonymous: EA is a 12 Step program for people who want to feel better. There may be an "Anonymous" group near you that can offer you much needed support.

SELF-TALK

What I focus on I will drift toward, create or attract! Today I will focus on how I can be good to myself.

Day 30

Abundant Life

Let Life be abundant for me and for all people! Amen.

It really is OK to love yourself
(in fact, it feels great!).

A Course in Miracles teaches love, forgiveness, and non-judgment. Many people have found the ACIM philosophy to be very healing in their lives. Is there an *A Course in Miracles* group near you?

SELF-TALK

What I focus on I will drift toward, create or attract! Today I will focus on forgiving myself and others for mistakes, real or imagined. As I let go of the past, I am free to create a joyous future.

Day 31

Good is Always Possible

I look beyond appearances to the Truth that Good is always possible.

You have amazing potential. You are not your past. You are not the judgments others have made. You are not your mistakes. You are divine Life in expression, and there are wonderful opportunities available to you. You deserve to be happy and there are many joyous experiences just waiting for you.

SELF-TALK

What I focus on I will drift toward, create or attract! Today I will focus on what makes my heart glad.

Additional Prayers:

Blessing Others

Dear God, when I think of one who is hurting, who is scared, who is feeling alone, who is confused, who is overwhelmed, I want to touch that person with the healing power of your love. When I think lovingly of such a person, may your grace flow immediately into her/his life, offering all that is needed for that person to feel whole, safe, optimistic, and truly happy. Amen.

SELF-TALK: I know what it feels like to need kindness, and so I give kindness freely to someone who needs it today.

Finances

Wisdom is guiding me now to make good financial decisions. There are wonderful opportunities for me and I am making the most of them. As I am blessed, I bless others, and as I prosper, I am very generous. I give thanks for divine Abundance which is being made manifest in my life right now. And so it is.

SELF-TALK: I'm prosperous because I have something to share!

For a Depressed Loved One

Healing Love, I see how this precious one aches, and I wish her/his heart to be lifted up, right now. May the veil of depression be lifted so that s/he can see the beauty of life, the good qualities within her/him, and the healing possibilities that are ever present. I bless this dear one now and I affirm hope, healing, and happiness for her/him in the name of all that is good and holy. Amen.

SELF-TALK: My love and compassion can make a real difference in someone's life!

Forgiveness

Wherever I am holding self-judgment, self-condemnation, shame, guilt, regret, or fear and wherever and whenever I have failed to let myself love myself, may I now be willing to forgive myself. Forgiveness is a healing power, and I am so ready to be healed. Amen.

When I bring to my mind someone who hurt me intentionally or by accident, in ways that were real or imagined, I will quickly say these healing words: ***Sacred Power, with your help I forgive this person, and I allow myself to remember that s/he is a child of your unconditional and eternal love. Let me now be healed from the pain, not only of her/his actions, but also the pain I have caused myself by judging her/him, and by not being willing to forgive until now. Touch us both, and let each of us now receive a miracle. Amen.***

SELF-TALK: I can release the past and let it go. I am free to create a bright future.

Grief

I am feeling the sadness that comes from profound loss. I trust that grief is a healing process and my joy will be restored. Until then, may angels hold me close, and bless my memories, and lead me ever forward in the ways of comfort, strength, and progress. Amen.

SELF-TALK: Grief isn't weakness; it is a healing process.

Healing

I know that healing can happen in an instant. Could it be this instant? I am open and receptive to my healing now, however it may come. Amen.

SELF TALK: Healing is possible!!!

Love

I am loveable. I deserve love in my life. I am loving. I am loved. *I am love.* This truth brings me joy and all things are working together for my highest good. Amen.

SELF-TALK: I am more loved than I realize. As I love myself more, I discover how much love there is in the world for me.

Peace

Fill our hearts with peace, O God; and as people filled with peace, may we contribute to peace in our world. Amen.

SELF-TALK: I deserve to experience peace within.

Self Esteem

I am made in the divine image, filled with the spirit of life, and I am part of a world that is very good. I am one with all the genius, all the beauty, all the love, all the kindness, all the courage, and all the wisdom that ever has been and ever will be. I am a miracle! How could I have ever forgotten such an important truth? Well, today I remember. Today I declare it to be so! Today I celebrate who I am and for the gift that I am to the world, I give thanks. Amen.

SELF-TALK: I have amazing potential; I really do!

Starting Over

Here I am again, God! Haven't I settled this issue already? Haven't I taken care of this business before? Apparently, I have more to do. I will not judge myself, nor will I feel sad. I am choosing to be grateful that I have another opportunity to make more progress. This is a healing moment. I'm ready for a miracle. Amen.

SELF-TALK: It's OK to be where I am and who I am.

 **Rev. Dr. Durrell Watkins** is the Senior Minister at Sunshine Cathedral in Fort Lauderdale, FL (www.sunshinecathedral.org).

BA, Henderson State University
MA, Goddard College
MDiv, Union Theological Seminary
DMin, Episcopal Divinity School

Other books by Dr. Watkins (all available at Amazon.com):

Wrestling With God Without Getting Pinned: Old Stories, New Thoughts, & Progressive Spirituality

Optimism & Gratitude: Prayers for Every Day of the Year

Progressive, Positive, & Practical: New Thought Reflections

Fairy Dust: Using Affirmations to Unlock the Magic of Life

A Treatment A Day (a book of and about prayer)

www.ingramcontent.com/pod-product-compliance
Ingram Content Group UK Ltd.
Pitfield, Milton Keynes, MK11 3LW, UK
UKHW020219250726
13967UKWH00001B/80

9 780557 865154